A New True Book

WEEDS AND WILD FLOWERS

By Illa Podendorf

This "true book" was prepared
under the direction of
Illa Podendorf,
formerly with the Laboratory School,
University of Chicago

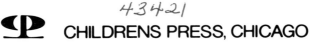

CHILDRENS PRESS, CHICAGO

Mayapple

PHOTO CREDITS

James P. Rowan—cover, 2, 4, 6, 9 (2), 10, 11 (2), 13 (3), 14 (4), 15 (2), 16, 18 (2), 22, 25, 26, 29, 31 (3), 32 (bottom), 34, 35 (left), 36 (3), 37 (4), 38 (4), 39 (3), 40, 41 (3), 42 (4), 43 (2), 45
Lynn M. Stone—9 (top), 12, 32 (top), 35 (right), 36 (bottom right), 41 (middle left), 44
Courtesy, Field Museum of Natural History, Chicago—7, 17, 21
James Benton—20, 24
Cover—Black-eyed Susan

Library of Congress Cataloging in Publication Data

Podendorf, Illa.
  Weeds and wild flowers.

  (A New true book)
  Previously published as: The true book of
weeds and wild flowers. 1955.
  SUMMARY: An introduction to weeds that are
always "weeds" and weeds that are considered
wild flowers.
  1. Weeds—Juvenile literature.   2. Wild
flowers—Juvenile literature.   [1. Weeds.
2. Wild flowers]   I. Title.
SB611.P58   1981   632'.58   81-7737
ISBN 0-516-01661-X   AACR2

TABLE OF CONTENTS

Dandelions in seed

PLANTS THAT ARE WEEDS

A weed is a plant. It grows where it is not wanted. Plants that are wanted are not weeds.

People like plants when they grow in the right places. Most people do not like weeds. Weeds grow in the wrong places.

Red Clover

We like grass in our
yards. We like clover in
our clover fields. We do
not like grass and clover
in our gardens.

People do not usually plant weeds. Weeds plant their own seeds. The wind pushes a tumbleweed along the ground. The tumbleweed plants its seeds as it goes along.

Tumbleweed

Sunflowers are some-of-the-time weeds. They are weeds when they grow in cornfields. They are wild flowers when they grow along a road. When we plant them in our gardens, sunflowers are garden flowers.

Sunflower

Tickseed Sunflower

Mule Ears Sunflower

Giant Ragweed

Ragweed is an all-of-the-time weed. Almost no one ever wants it around. It causes many people to have hay fever.

Mouse-ear Chickweed   Violet Wood Sorrel

WEEDS OF THE LAWN

These plants are often
called weeds of the lawn.
They could have a
different name. They could
be called lawn flowers.
Since these plants are not
wanted, they are weeds.

11

Dandelion

Dandelions are weeds of the lawn.

These weeds grow and grow. Their flowers are not very pretty.

Far left:
Field Thistle

Left:
Mullein

Below:
Queen Anne's
Lace

WEEDS OF THE ROADSIDE

These weeds could be called flowers of the roadside.

Wild carrot is also called Queen Anne's lace.

Common Milkweed

Common Milkweed pods

Giant Ragweed

Common Yarrow

All these weeds plant
their own seeds.

Foxtail

Wild Barley

The weeds on this page
are in the grass family.
They grow along the
roadside, too.

St. John's Wort

WEEDS OF THE GARDEN

Some weeds have pretty
flowers. Even so, weeds
are not wanted in gardens.

Sandbur and quack grass are weeds in the grass family.

Peppergrass looks like grass. So does Shepherd's purse.

But they are not in the grass family. They are in the mustard family.

Sandbur

Hoary Vervain

Wild Mustard

WEEDS OF THE FIELDS

These weeds could be called flowers of the fields. Mustard often grows in grain fields.

Smartweed

Smartweed is sometimes called lady's thumb.
Velvetleaf has heart-shaped leaves.

Cocklebur

Burdock and cocklebur
seeds have sticky
coverings. The seeds catch
rides on the hair of
animals.

Poison Ivy

WEEDS OF THE WOODS

Many weeds grow in the woods.

This weed is poison ivy. Stay away from it. If it touches your skin, it will make it red and itchy.

It is easy to know poison ivy. Each leaf has three leaflets. Poison ivy has white berries, too.

Catnip

Catnip could be called a flower of the woods. Cats like catnip.

We often get the seeds of Spanish needles on our clothes as we walk through woods.

Indian Hemp

WEEDS DO HARM

Weeds can hurt other
kinds of plants. They take
food and water from the
soil.

Bindweed

Some weeds grow tall.
They keep the sun away
from other plants.

Some weeds hang onto
other plants.

They pull the plants
down.

This is how to get rid of weeds. Pull weeds up by the roots. Hoe gardens carefully. Plow fields well. Stop weeds from making seeds. Plant seeds that have no weed seeds among them.

Cream False Indigo

Sometimes weeds do good instead of harm. They may keep the soil from being washed away by water.

PLANTS THAT ARE WILD FLOWERS

All of the plants in this book have flowers. Some of them have pretty flowers. We like plants that have pretty flowers. We call these plants wild flowers instead of weeds because we like them.

Left: Butterfly Weed
Below left: Purple Coneflower
Below right: Close-up of
           Purple Coneflower

Purple coneflowers are
called wild flowers.

Hepatica

Hepatica

WILD FLOWERS
OF EARLY SPRING

Hepatica is one of spring's first wild flowers. It may bloom when snow is still on the ground.

Bloodroot

Many wild flowers need
to be protected because
there are very few of them
left.

Common Blue Violet

Violets are of different
colors. They can be purple,
lavender, white, or yellow.

Jack-in-the-Pulpit

Wild Columbine

Here are other kinds of
wild flowers to look for.

Spiderwort

Spring Beauty

Mountain Buttercup

Bluebells

Wild Geranium

37

Dutchman's Breeches

Mayapple

Bluets

Shooting Star

Trailing Arbutus

False Rue Anemone

White Trillium

Spring wild flowers never grow very tall. They usually have pale colors.

Wild Blue Phlox

Aster

WILD FLOWERS OF SUMMER AND FALL

Many summer wild
flowers have bright colors.
Summer wild flowers
usually grow taller than
spring wild flowers do.

Top left: Black-eyed Susan
Middle left: Fringed Gentian
Bottom left: Ox-eye Daisies
Above: Lupine

Above: Day Lily
Right: Evening Primrose
Below left: Canada Goldenrod
Below right: Indian Paintbrush

Wild Rose

Carolina Rose

Wild roses are pretty blossoms. They grow on bushes.

SAVE WILD FLOWERS

If we do not try to save wild flowers soon they will all be gone. There are very few lady's slippers left, because people have not tried to save them.

Lady's Slipper

Do not pick wild flowers.
Do not dig them up. Tell
other people to take care
of wild flowers, too.

WORDS YOU SHOULD KNOW

berry(BER • ee)—the fruit of some plants

blossom—flower

clover(KLO • ver)—a plant which has three leaflets

flower(FLOU • er)—the part of a plant that makes seeds

grain(GRAYN)—the seed of wheat, corn, rice, and other plants
    used to make cereal

grass—a green plant with narrow leaves

hay fever(HAY fee • ver)—a condition of running nose and
    watering eyes caused by a part of a plant

hoe(HOH)—a hand tool used to break up soil

lawn—ground where grass grows; yard

leaflet(LEEF • let)—a small leaf

pale—not bright, dull

plant(n)—a living thing that is not an animal

plant (v)—to put into soil to grow

plow—to break up soil

protect(proh • TEKT)—keep safe; guard

root—the part of a plant that grows into the soil

seed—the part of the plant that grows into a new plant

soil—the top layer of the earth's surface where plants grow; earth

INDEX

About the Author

Born and raised in western Iowa, Illa has had experience teaching science at both elementary and high school levels. For many years she served as head of Science Dept., Laboratory School, University of Chicago and is currently consultant on the series of True Books and author of many of them. A pioneer in creative teaching, she has been especially successful in working with the gifted child.

434.21

S-2/11 206/06 9 circs 7 libs